▶ YouTubers

NINJA

JESSICA RUSICK

Checkerboard
Library

An Imprint of Abdo Publishing
abdobooks.com

abdobooks.com

Published by Abdo Publishing, a division of ABDO, PO Box 398166, Minneapolis, Minnesota 55439. Copyright © 2020 by Abdo Consulting Group, Inc. International copyrights reserved in all countries. No part of this book may be reproduced in any form without written permission from the publisher. Checkerboard Library™ is a trademark and logo of Abdo Publishing.

Printed in the United States of America, North Mankato, Minnesota
102019
012020

 THIS BOOK CONTAINS
RECYCLED MATERIALS

Design: Sarah DeYoung, Mighty Media, Inc.
Production: Mighty Media, Inc.
Editor: Rebecca Felix
Cover Photograph: Shutterstock Images
Interior Photographs: Bago Games/Flickr, pp. 7, 19, 29 (top); Bloomberg/Getty Images, p. 23; Ethan Miller/Getty Images, p. 27; Mighty Media, Inc., p. 25 (middle, bottom); Shutterstock Images, pp. 5, 17, 21, 25 (top), 28, 29 (bottom); Tarcil Tarcil/Flickr, p. 11; Tess_Trunk/iStockphoto, pp. 6, 16, 22, 24, 25, 28, 29; Wikimedia Commons, pp. 9, 15; ZUMA Press, Inc./Alamy Stock Photo, p. 13

Library of Congress Control Number: 2019943325

Publisher's Cataloging-in-Publication Data
Names: Rusick, Jessica, author.
Title: Ninja / by Jessica Rusick
Description: Minneapolis, Minnesota : Abdo Publishing, 2020 | Series: YouTubers | Includes online resources and index.
Identifiers: ISBN 9781532191824 (lib. bdg.) | ISBN 9781644943601 (pbk.) | ISBN 9781532178559 (ebook)
Subjects: LCSH: Ninja (eSports gamer), 1991- (Richard Blevins)--Biography--Juvenile literature. | YouTube (Firm)--Juvenile literature. | Video game players (Persons)--Biography--Juvenile literature. | Internet celebrities--Biography--Juvenile literature. | Streaming video--Juvenile literature. | Internet videos--Juvenile literature. | Fortnite Battle Royale (Game)--Juvenile literature.
Classification: DDC 794.8092--dc23

NOTE TO READERS

Video games that depict shooting or other violent acts should be subject to adult discretion and awareness that exposure to such acts may affect players' perceptions of violence in the real world.

Contents

Get to Know Ninja

Ninja is a YouTube star and competitive gamer. He records himself playing video games and posts videos of this gameplay online. His YouTube channel, Ninja, has more than 22 million **subscribers**!

Ninja got his start **streaming** gaming videos on the website Twitch. He posted **highlights** of his Twitch videos on YouTube. Ninja became known for his gaming talent. He also became known for his personality. In Ninja's videos, he often talks to viewers, cracks jokes, and does funny impressions while playing.

For years, Ninja was a successful YouTuber. But he became a social media star in 2017. This is when Ninja started playing the popular video game *Fortnite*. Ninja's gaming talents have earned him millions of fans and millions of dollars. He is often called the face of modern gaming.

Ninja is an inspiration to young gamers. His passion began when he too was young. Ninja grew up playing video games against his older brothers.

Ninja has turned his name and his gaming skills into a brand. He produces clothing, books, and other merchandise.

Kid Gamer

Richard Tyler "Ninja" Blevins was born on June 5, 1991, in Taylor, Michigan. He went by his middle name. Tyler's parents are Chuck and Cynthia. Tyler has two older brothers, John and Chris. When Tyler was a baby, the family moved from Michigan to Grayslake, Illinois.

Tyler was exposed to video games from a young age. His dad was an **avid** gamer. So, Tyler's house had many gaming consoles. These included a Super Nintendo, Sony PlayStation, and Microsoft Xbox. Tyler and his brothers loved to play games on these consoles.

Cynthia did not want her sons to spend too much time playing video games. So, she let them play only if they followed certain rules. One was that for every hour the boys gamed, they had to spend one hour playing outdoors.

In November 2001, the futuristic war game *Halo: Combat Evolved* came out on Xbox. Players could

Halo: *Combat Evolved* follows a soldier fighting an evil alien race.

play this game by themselves. They could also play in several multiplayer modes.

Halo soon became Tyler and his brothers' favorite game. At ten years old, Tyler was a naturally skilled gamer. He often won games against his older brothers!

From Novice to Ninja

Tyler's love of gaming grew as he got older. In November 2004, a second *Halo* game came out. Tyler played this game against gamers worldwide through Xbox Live.

Competing against Xbox Live players made Tyler aware of his talent. His opponents included professional video gamers, or eSports players. And Tyler sometimes beat them!

Tyler saw that eSport players traveled the country competing in video game tournaments. He wondered if he too could play in these tournaments. But as a teen, Tyler was busy with school. In 2005, he began attending Grayslake Central High School. In his spare time, Tyler continued gaming on Xbox Live.

In June 2009, Tyler turned 18 and graduated high school. That same month, he attended his first video gaming tournament, Major League Gaming (MLG), in Columbus, Ohio.

Tyler played *Halo 3* in the tournament with a team of three other gamers. Like all competitors, Tyler played under a screen name. He chose "Ninja." This was the name of a player

Competitive video gaming tournaments draw large crowds of fans who watch players compete on large screens.

action in *Halo*. Ninja's team played against 217 other teams and ranked within the top 64 teams. As someone new to competitive gaming, Ninja felt happy with this result.

Streaming Success

Ninja had entered the world of video game tournaments. But he still focused on his schooling. In 2009, he began attending Silver Lake College in Manitowoc, Wisconsin. Ninja got a job at a Noodles & Co. fast-food restaurant. When he wasn't in class, studying, or working, he gamed.

In June 2010, Ninja's gaming team returned to MLG Columbus and placed 25th! One year later, Ninja found a new platform for his gaming. In June 2011, Twitch launched. It allows gamers to **stream** videos of themselves gaming. Viewers watch the gameplay as it happens.

Ninja began streaming himself playing *Halo: Reach*, the sixth game in the Halo series. A large screen showed Ninja's character in the game. A small screen within the larger one showed Ninja playing the game in real time.

Twitch allowed fans to send Ninja questions and comments as he played using a live chat room. Ninja read and responded to these out loud while he played.

Ninja earned a growing following on Twitch. Around the same time as his Twitch **debut**, Ninja decided to quit his job and leave Silver Lake College. He enrolled in a community college closer to home to save money. The community college had a cheaper tuition than Silver Lake College.

Twitch has more than 9 million channels!

Back home in Illinois, Ninja got another job at a local Noodles & Co. Outside of class and work, he gamed and posted on Twitch as much as possible. Ninja would often **stream** for ten hours at a time!

Ninja's parents worried about how much time their son spent streaming. They believed gaming could never be more than a hobby. But Ninja would soon prove them wrong.

By November 2011, Ninja had 220 Twitch **subscribers** and 10,000 followers. Being a follower was free on Twitch. But the service also gave viewers the option to pay for a subscription. The subscription gave them access to a certain chat room and special **emoticons** that could be posted there.

Ninja earned a portion of the money Twitch brought in from paid subscriptions. Fans could also **donate** money directly to Ninja. In 2011, Ninja was earning about $100 a day streaming on Twitch.

Now that Ninja was earning money from gaming, he left his restaurant job to devote more time to Twitch. Ninja stayed in school, though. He felt it was important to have a solid education in case his gaming career didn't work out.

Ninja (*front*) competes in a gaming tournament in 2011.

YouTube Noob

Though Ninja had doubts that his gaming career would continue to grow, it did just that! In 2011, Ninja expanded his platform by launching a YouTube channel. He uploaded his first YouTube videos on December 15.

Many of Ninja's YouTube videos were shorter versions of his Twitch videos. On Twitch, Ninja often **streamed** for hours at a time. But most of his YouTube posts were under 12 minutes long. This is because Ninja's YouTube videos showed only the **highlights** from his Twitch streams.

Ninja's highlights often included moves that the average gamer could not complete. Fans admired Ninja's talent. They also liked his personality. Ninja talked to viewers during his hours-long Twitch streams. He made jokes, quoted lines from TV shows, and did funny impressions. He included much of this commentary in his YouTube videos.

Ninja also shared advice in his videos on how to become a successful Twitch streamer. He explained how to create a

Gaming content gained popularity in the years following Twitch's launch. In 2015, YouTube created the app YouTube Gaming to compete with video game streaming platforms.

personal connection with Twitch fans. Ninja felt it was important to talk to fans and answer questions while **streaming**. This helped viewers feel they were part of the gaming process.

Some of Ninja's advice was for young gamers who wanted to compete in eSports. By sharing this advice, Ninja hoped to support the dreams of a future generation of gamers.

By October 2012, Ninja had 10,000 YouTube **subscribers**. And Ninja was gaining fans on Twitch too. In late 2012, he had close to 20,000 followers on this platform! He also had many paying subscribers on Twitch.

Soon, Ninja was making $80,000 a year from his **streamed** games. His gaming career had become steady and successful. Ninja decided to leave school to focus on gaming full-time.

In 2013, Ninja began **vlogging** on YouTube. In his vlogs, Ninja gave his viewers life updates. This included when he would be playing in tournaments. That way, fans would know when he would be traveling and could not stream. They would also know when to watch tournaments online.

Ninja continued to play in Halo competitions until 2017. In November 2012, his team took first place at the MLG Fall Championships. They received a prize of $20,000!

That same year, Ninja developed a closer connection with one of his fans, Jessica Goch. Ninja met Goch at an eSports tournament in 2010. Three years later, the two began dating.

Jessica Goch is also a gamer! When playing online games, she goes by the screen name JGhosty.

Battle Royale

By 2014, Ninja had a sizeable Twitch and YouTube following. On August 13, he reached 1,000 paid Twitch **subscribers**. His YouTube channel had nearly 40,000 subscribers. But then, Ninja's growing career faced a setback.

Just days after reaching 1,000 Twitch subscribers, Ninja injured the **retina** in his right eye. Recovery would take about one month. During this time, Ninja could not play video games. He announced this news on YouTube on August 15. Because he could not **stream**, Ninja lost Twitch followers. Ninja feared this injury might slow his gaming career.

In September, Ninja began posting again on Twitch and YouTube. He soon bounced back from his absence. By January 2015, Ninja's Twitch follower count reached 100,000! Later that year, he found success with a new style of game.

On a friend's recommendation, Ninja started playing battle royale games. Many people play battle royale games at once. Their online characters battle until one player is left standing.

PlayerUnknown's Battlegrounds is credited for making battle royale games widely popular.

Ninja soon became hooked on battle royale games. He began posting videos of him playing two of them, called *H1Z1* and *PlayerUnknown's Battlegrounds*.

Tens of thousands of viewers watched Ninja's battle royale Twitch **streams**. And each YouTube **highlights** video of these streams earned hundreds of thousands of views! Soon, one battle royale game would help Ninja's fame skyrocket.

Fortnite Phenom

Into 2017, Ninja continued posting videos of battle royale games. He also continued dating Goch. That August, the two married! Ninja took a six-day break from **streaming** to take a **honeymoon** to the Caribbean.

When Ninja returned from his honeymoon, he got back to gaming. While reading fan comments on Twitch in September, he noticed many were talking about *Fortnite*.

Fortnite was a new online battle royale game. One *Fortnite* game involved 100 players. In the game, each player's character is dropped onto an island. Then, the characters battle until only one player is left standing. In October, Ninja decided to give the game a try.

Ninja was one of the first major Twitch users to stream *Fortnite*. The game grew in popularity in coming months. So did Ninja's popularity. **Highlights** of his Twitch *Fortnite* streams were a hit on YouTube. By early 2018, Ninja had more than 4 million followers on YouTube.

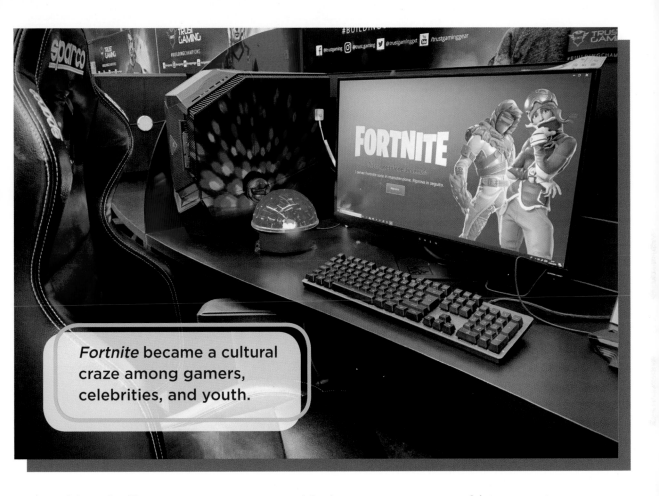

Fortnite became a cultural craze among gamers, celebrities, and youth.

Ninja's *Fortnite* content quickly became some of his most popular on YouTube. Some *Fortnite* games he played solo. Others he played as a team, or duo. Ninja teamed up with other gamers and even celebrities for these games!

On March 14, 2018, Ninja played several *Fortnite* duos alongside star rapper Drake. Drake learned of Ninja's *Fortnite* videos and became a fan. Soon after, Drake messaged Ninja over social media asking to play *Fortnite* together. Ninja agreed.

Though Drake and Ninja played *Fortnite* as a team, they were in different physical locations. The pair spoke to one another through a headset.

During the games, Drake and Ninja worked to eliminate other players. Later that night, they expanded their team! Rapper Travis Scott and football player JuJu Smith-Schuster joined Ninja and Drake as teammates for one *Fortnite* game.

Ninja's star-studded *Fortnite* **stream** broke records on Twitch. At its peak, more than 600,000 viewers watched the stream! The previous Twitch record was 388,000 viewers.

Following Ninja's game day with Drake, many news outlets ran stories about Ninja's rise to fame. Many called him the face of modern gaming and eSports. The media attention boosted Ninja's popularity. By April, his YouTube **subscriber** count reached nearly 10 million. Ninja credited Drake's popularity for helping increase his own.

Ninja often dyes his hair different colors. In the past, his hair has been bright green and bright pink!

Ninja takes a selfie with fans at a 2018 *Fortnite* tournament.

Tournament Time

Ninja was more popular than ever. In April 2018, HyperX eSports arena in Las Vegas, Nevada, held a tournament in his honor! There, fans and top gamers competed against Ninja in *Fortnite*. Ninja **streamed** the tournament on Twitch. It received 680,000 live views. This beat the record he set with Drake.

In June, Ninja competed in a *Fortnite* tournament in Los Angeles, California. There, famous gamers and other stars played in teams of two to win money for **charities**. Ninja's teammate was a celebrity **disc jockey** who goes by the name Marshmello. The duo won $1 million at the tournament. Ninja **donated** his portion to the **Alzheimer's** Association.

VIP Post

Ninja's most popular YouTube video shows him eliminating 32 players during a *Fortnite* game. The video has been viewed more than 40 million times!

New Channels

Clothing: In September 2018, Ninja launched a clothing and **merchandise** line. Many items feature Ninja's cartoon logo of a blue face wearing a yellow **bandanna**.

Music: In December 2018, Ninja worked on a music album called *Ninjawerks: Vol. 1.* Ninja chose the songs for the album. Some were inspired by video games! Clips of Ninja speaking is used as the background of one song.

Book: In August 2019, Ninja released a book. *Ninja: Get Good: My Ultimate Guide to Gaming* shares tips on improving gaming skills.

Gaming earned Ninja money that he kept too. In addition to money from Twitch **subscribers**, Ninja made money by **promoting** brands on Twitch and YouTube. This earned Ninja about $500,000 a month!

Gaming Role Model

Ninja told his fans how much money he made gaming. He wanted to show young gamers that a successful career in gaming was possible. Ninja hoped that one day, eSports gaming would become as **mainstream** as traditional sports.

In the fall of 2018, another accomplishment of Ninja's supported this goal. It also made history. Ninja became the first gamer featured on the cover of the sports-themed *ESPN the Magazine*. He appears in the October issue.

In August 2019, Ninja's popularity was at an all-time high. He had more than 22 million YouTube followers! That same month, Ninja made a big change. He left Twitch to **stream** exclusively on the similar platform Mixer. In just five days, Ninja had 1 million Mixer **subscribers**!

Ninja continued to play *Fortnite* in 2019. But he said he may stop in the future, as he did not want to be known for just the game.

Instead, Ninja hoped to be known for making eSports more popular. "I want to be remembered as the grandfather of gaming," he said. Game on!

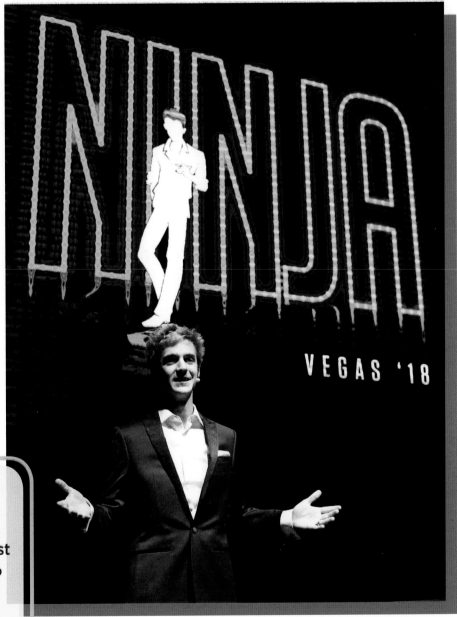

In 2019, the *Los Angeles Times* called Ninja "the most popular video game player in the world."

Timeline

1991

Richard Tyler "Ninja" Blevins is born on June 5 in Taylor, Michigan. He goes by Tyler.

2004

Halo 2 is released in November. Tyler plays this game on Xbox Live.

2011

Ninja begins streaming his gameplay on Twitch in June. In December, he makes a YouTube channel.

2001

Halo: Combat Evolved is released in November. Tyler plays this game with his older brothers.

2009

Tyler attends his first gaming tournament. He plays under the name Ninja.

2015

Ninja begins playing battle royale games.

2018

In March, Ninja plays *Fortnite* with celebrities. The streams set a Twitch record for most views.

2018

Ninja is the first professional gamer to appear on the cover of *ESPN the Magazine*, in the October issue.

2013

Ninja posts his first YouTube vlogs. He begins dating Jessica Goch.

2017

Ninja marries Goch in August. In October, he begins streaming *Fortnite*.

2018

Ninja hosts and competes in a *Fortnite* tournament in April. His Twitch stream of it breaks his previous record for most views.

Glossary

Alzheimer's—an illness that causes forgetfulness, confusion, and overall mental disintegration.

avid—enthusiastic or eager.

bandanna—a large, colorful handkerchief that can be worn around the head or neck.

charity—a group or fund that helps people in need.

debut (DAY-byoo)—a first appearance.

disc jockey—a person who plays or remixes recorded music for dancing at a night club, concert, or party.

donate—to give.

emoticon—a small image of a face expressing some emotion, used in email, in apps, and online to communicate a feeling or attitude.

highlight—an important or interesting part of something.

honeymoon—a trip or vacation taken by a newly married couple.

mainstream—relating to the ideas, attitudes, activities, or trends that are regarded as normal or dominant in society.

merchandise—goods that are bought and sold.

promote—to contribute to the growth, prosperity, or popularity of an item, brand, or person through advertising or support.

retina—the lining at the back of the eyeball that sends images to a person's brain.

stream—to transfer data, such as video, in a steady stream so it can be watched or played immediately. This video is called a stream.

subscriber—someone who signs up to receive something on a regular basis. A subscription is the right to receive something, sometimes obtained by paying in advance.

vlog—a video log that tells about someone's personal opinions, activities, and experiences. To vlog is to create these video logs.

Online Resources

Booklinks
NONFICTION NETWORK
FREE! ONLINE NONFICTION RESOURCES

To learn more about Ninja, please visit **abdobooklinks.com** or scan this QR code. These links are routinely monitored and updated to provide the most current information available.

Index